T0129990

Chiseled InTelliGeNcE

A Book of Inspiration Volume 1

(A MUST READ & MUST KEEP BOOK OF INSPIRATION)

George D. Naike, F.R.C., MCIH.

BALBOA.
PRESS
A DIVISION OF HAY HOUSE

Balboa Press books may be ordered through booksellers or by contacting:

Balboa Press
A Division of Hay House
1663 Liberty Drive
Bloomington, IN 47403
www.balboapress.com.au
1 (877) 407-4847

Print information available on the last page.

ISBN: 978-1-5043-0213-5 (sc)
ISBN: 978-1-5043-0214-2 (e)

Balboa Press rev. date: 05/04/2016

Preamble

The author believes that humanity, in its evolution, will advance well through acts of generosity, love and kindness toward nature and one another, regardless of race, religion, political persuasion, ability …

Acknowledgement

This book is dedicated to every person who defies all odds to achieve their dream.

Gratitude

Thank you to my wife, Michelle, and
our two daughters, Elizabeth and Sarah
for their support and understanding
during the creation of this book.

'Chiseled Intelligence'©.

Unique quotes crafted
from inspired thoughts.

"Today is phenomenal.
It is changing into yesterday and by subtlety also turning into tomorrow's history."

(Dedicated to all those living positively today)

"Nothing was until made be.
Think creatively."

(Dedicated to creative thinkers worldwide)

George D. Naike, F.R.C., MCIH.

"The happiness of humanity depends on each person. Do your share."

(Dedicated to spirit uplifted)

"Within each of us lie answers to all life's questions, which can be heard through silence. Listen to your conscience. The human Conscience is a 'Surround
System' by nature. It guides our thoughts, words and actions. It is always asking for the right reasons."

(Dedicated to the conscientious)

Geоrge D. Naike, F.R.C., MCIH.

"Memories are made of each
moment we live to experience.
Cherish every moment of your life."

"Silver, Gold and Diamonds are dead cheap compared to wisdom. Choose wisely."

George D. Naike, F.R.C., MCIH.

"Genuine excellence is the self less habits
of kindness toward others, especially
those less privileged."

(Dedicated to Oprah Winfrey)

"Appointment remains when 'Dis' is not regarded. Be optimistic."

George D. Naike, F.R.C., MCIH.

"If you're strong use your strength
to positively lift up the weak."

(Dedicated to givers of care worldwide)

"If you are invited,
be an excellent guest."

(Dedicated to good guests)

George D. Naike, F.R.C., MCIH.

"Pictures, right numbers and carefully selected words surely make things happen."

(Dedicated to Pictures, Theatres, Actors & Actresses)

"Naturally you receive when you give,
but the best is the latter. Give
all and all will surely give you.
The rewards of giving are
amazingly relentless."

(Dedicated to the generous and the giving)

George D. Naike, F.R.C., MCIH.

"The use of sensible reticence before reaching any point of impact is undoubtedly wise."

"Intangible to the looking eyes but the effects of air are undeniable. Nature serves it fresh and freely, breath and see."

(Dedicated to Nature)

George D. Naike, F.R.C., MCIH.

"Habits take root in the repetition of any behaviour we train the mind to accept. Every habit therefore is equally reversible. Use the power of your Freewill for change."

(Dedicated to anyone positively trying to adopt or give up a habit)

"Up and down or give and take are a good start to freely think in different dimensions."

(Dedicated to Sir Isaac Newton of the Gravity fame)

GEORGE D. NAIKE, F.R.C., MCIH.

"Each day is a successful page of learning when peacefully turned."

(Dedicated to Alfred Noble of the Nobel Peace Price fame and every worthy recipient)

"If words are ships air is surely the only ocean by which they can sail."

(Dedicated to World Media, Journalism
and all good Journalists)

"If the world is to be your judge,
the best-compelling case
you can ever put forward is that of
honesty shrouded in humility."

(Dedicated to Justice, the Legal
Profession & Legal Practitioners)

"Meaningful has meaning, wisdom has wise. Chisel your words thoroughly and mean them wisely as said."

(Dedicated to Philosophy and Philosophers, past and present)

George D. Naike, F.R.C., MCIH.

"Goodwill is the sure and unassailable imperative, the world over.
Where genuine goodwill beckons, other imperatives must wait."

(Dedicated in goodwill to humanity)

"The truth is one dimensional.
It is, or not. Ask a good lawyer."

(Dedicated to my mentor, Kay Scudder)

"Every lifetime is a lesson learned.
Live and learn."

(Dedicated to life lessons)

"The human intellect has
phenomenal potential when placed
in the right advantage."

(Dedicated to development of self and others)

George D. Naike, F.R.C., MCIH.

"True Love is incontrovertible.
Everyone deserves its effects."

(Dedicated to anyone searching for love)

"Maturity is thinking as you will and speaking as you think in the instance."

(Dedicated to Kyle D. Sandilands - Kiis 106.5, Australia)

"The wealth of wisdom elude even some of the so-called wealthy. The combination of Money and affluence does not mean automatic wisdom."

(Dedicated to the wealthy and truly benevolent)

"You stop time when you deliver joy into the heart of humanity. For that single reason, time will remind humanity of you, even when you're long gone. Leave your mark."

(Dedicated to Vera Randall of Knitwit - Australia's Inaugural Business Woman of the Year and her husband, Mike Padden, affectionately known as the Grandfather of Franchising)

"A hero with good morals
is the true such."

(Dedicated to Australians of the Year and Persons
of the Year in the countries of the world)

"Time may be money, but money is certainly not time. The distinction is clear, one controls the other."

(Dedicated to those who value time)

"To be wise, one must be prepared to accept that strangely good things happen to wise people."

(Dedicated to seekers of wisdom)

"If it occupies space and has
weight, then it matters."

(Dedicated to Science and all Scientists worldwide)

Gᴇᴏʀɢᴇ D. Nᴀɪᴋᴇ, F.R.C., MCIH.

"If you can perform it,
you can profess it."

(Dedicated to all defenders of education)

"When you read, you share some form of history."

(Dedicated to book lovers worldwide)

"Without balance, surely there is bias."

"Be structured, be measured and you're sure to be amazed."

"I am today whom I was not yesterday, change tells me. Good change should speak in clear enough decibels, pay attention and take benefit."

"When you think of the above, naturally you are looking up. Aim High."

(Dedicated to those pursuing or living their dreams)

"Peace of mind is a rare commodity,
primarily attained at no cost."

(Dedicated to Psychology, Psychologists, Psychiatry,
Psychiatrists, Inner Peace and Health to Mind)

"Never hold your breath for longer than
necessary, trust is a big thing."

"Some people you meet are in the world to help shape your life. The real asking is to recognise them when they show up and to take their advise like you're seeing them for the very last time."

(Dedicated to Simone Carson, Liam Chandler, Ann Sherwin and James Benson)

"True meditation is the complete and undivided focus on a particular matter in absolute quiet submission to the inner self. Relax in a quiet place and try it with your eyes closed."

(Dedicated to Inner Light)

"Technology has existed from time immemorial. We just prefer the ones of today because of how they charm and excite us, yet they become tomorrow's history."

(Dedicated to Architecture, Architects, The Built Environment, Builders, Engineering and Engineers)

"There goes time, our ubiquitous companion. So constant not even a broken clock brings it any knowing. Neither can the most advanced time-traveller argue with its 'Perpetual' constancy."

(Dedicated to Hans Wilsdorf of the Rolex fame)

"If rightly construed,
silence, in any form,
speaks louder than sound.
Dare I speak when I am
positively spoken for, and
dare I not when my words
might just inspire."

(Dedicated to motivational speeches)

"Focus, single-mindedness, centre, attention are useful for a common purpose, thinking."

(Dedicated to bearers of good thoughts)

George D. Naike, F.R.C., MCIH.

"Determination does lead to achievements, if we keep it in mind during the journey."

(Dedicated to my sister, Violet)

"Contentment is appreciating what you have, promising only what you can give and giving what you can afford."

(Dedicated to my parents)

"Incomparable intelligence sometimes comes from someone that the world never thought was gifted. Keep your talent and your dreams alive."

(Dedicated to Susan Boyle)

"The discernment of right and wrong
is crucial in the use of Free Will."

(Dedicated to those doing right)

"Your neighbour is not only
the one next door.
Positive thoughts shape
the world."

(Dedicated to those living at peace
with their neighbours).

"Love, Compassion, Kindness, Humility, Sincerity, Altruism ... are sure extensions of wisdom. To have it all is the true sower of all privileges."

(In memory of William Wilberforce)

"Without memories we cannot remember or reminisce. They journey us down those lanes which our waking state merely remember only to forget."

(Dedicated to Remembrance)

"True Love is fundamentally everything. It is old, it is young and it is unconditional. It is given and received freely since the beginning of time."

(Dedicated to lovers worldwide)

"Theory with no practice
is mere intellectual
pastime. Practicing make
experts."

(Dedicated to Albert Einstein)

"A wise person is one who learns
from not being one.
Wisdom is growing
change."

(Dedicated to growing up)

GEORGE D. NAIKE, F.R.C., MCIH.

"True pioneers are those who
focus particularly on creating,
developing and making 'it' work."

(Dedicated to Mark Zuckerberg, Sergei Brin,
Larry page and other pioneers of change
that positively advance humanity)

"No situation is the
worst unless we so make
it ."

(Dedicated to courage and the courageous)

"No other person sees things
the way you see them. Such
is the nature of diversity.
Variation is necessary, dialogue
will have no duty call if we all
reason same way at all times."

(Dedicated to solutions waiting for problems)

"To be happy and well are two things to be thankful for, but spare a feeling for those nurturing back to health. We rise on our feet once again through the support of our wonderful and yet passive heroes."

(Dedicated to Medicine and Medical Practitioners (Nurses and Paramedics included))

"Be positive and positivity will always seek you out. Positive and positivity are relative."

(Dedicated to positive thinkers)

"The true self can sometimes seem distant, but reality check brings it back to you."

"That never ending view of an offing over a beach definitely stretches the imagination, no matter how you see it."

(Dedicated to Lifeguards, Surfers, Beach Lovers and Sailors worldwide)

"'Allegory' serves to
communicate a
'literal nature' but the two
must never be confused."

(Dedicated to signs and symbols)

GEORGE D. NAIKE, F.R.C., MCIH.

"There is air in all, and all is in the Air.
Imagination brings me to
this conclusion."

(Dedicated to nature)

"It is possible to think without light.
However, bright and positive thoughts
lead us to illumination."

(Dedicated to true seekers of Inner Light)

GEORGE D. NAIKE, F.R.C., MCIH.

"As humans, we are fallible. However, the positive use of our free will is a good guidepost to perfecting our own nature."

(Dedicated to wilful acts of kindness)

"An unusual evolution that is difficult
for the human mind to comprehend
will result when our achievement
positively advances humanity."

(Dedicated to The United Nations and
all Humanitarians worldwide)

"The human memory is immensely powerful. It can reason and remember words, things, numbers, colours, images, tastes, smells, motion and even more."

(Dedicated to sensory awareness)

"The gift of imagination leads us to
create new from the unknown and also
to advance novelty
from that which already exists.
Such a gift it brings to just
imagine."

(Dedicated to inventors of things and intellectual
properties that positively advance humanity)

"Unquestioned answers delay progress in any discipline."

(Dedicated to Critics in all disciplines)

"If you show up for a meal without an appetite, you may just show yourself up. Eat well, drink sensibly and walk a stretch every so often."

(Live Life as best possible)

"We must teach children to excel in physical activities, to aspire to great things in life, and to reason and achieve intellectually, but by no means at the expense of inner health awareness."

(Dedicated to Mental Health)

"People are said to return to the "spirit world" when they pass away from the material realm. Does it sit logically then, that babies come from the "spirit world"?

(Dedicated to the Living)

Geᴏʀɢᴇ D. Nᴀɪᴋᴇ, F.R.C., MCIH.

"The word Love reverberates when said
meaningfully and even more
so when reciprocated.
It brings joy and
achieves wonders for
individuals, couples,
families and nations."

(Dedicated to families and those living
in domestic harmony worldwide)

"We transform into an epitome of goodness when our intentions are prompted from our inner nature."

(In memory of Robert Nesta Marley)

"Conscience and Intelligence are two worlds apart. Only an intelligent person with conscience can relate the two concepts successfully."

(Dedicated to The President of the United States of America, Barak Hussein Obama).

"Two right hands make a great handshake the world over."

(Dedicated to true friendship)

"A genius is the one who proposes an intellectual and moral material, then sustainably pursues and achieves excellence on that basis. Many more geniuses exist than we can ever care to count."

(Dedicated to ingenuity and talents awaiting discovery)

"In some circumstances, achievement of a single excellence may be greater than a lifetime of accolades."

(Dedicated to sports, sportsmanship and fair play)

"Practice giving and you will never be found wanting."

(Dedicated to Philanthropy and Philanthropists worldwide).

"One can only over-indulge if it is available."

(Dedicated to the moderate)

"The word sure is imperative.
Be sure to mean it
imperatively when you
say it."

(Dedicated to certainty and being certain)

"An illiterate is the teacher who confines education and success to only classroom activities."

(Dedicated to John McGrath of McGrath Real Estate, Australia)

"I think IQs fluctuate. We're not the same every moment of our waking state. Genius can only be timed, observed, captured and measured momentarily."

(Dedicated to Universal IQ)

"At the other end of each night there is a new day. At the end there is always a new start. Success is always ever anticipating discovery. Strife for it."

(Dedicated to Hope and the Hopeful)

GEORGE D. NAIKE, F.R.C., MCIH.

"The phenomenon of true love is that it remains forever. It never hangs in the balance."

(Dedicated to Love itself)

"'Common sense' is the sensation
of assimilated objective
perceptions. When properly called
into use, it brings 'real sense' to the
moment."

(Dedicated to the witty and the discerning)

"If you must carry the world shoulder high, you also need a torch to illuminate the path of life. For it is quite a journey."

(Dedicated to Loving Life)

"Sitting or standing,
the sun shines on us, regardless.
In its golden fashion, it makes no
exception, it shares with all its
glory."

(Dedicated to Equality)

"'Having' becomes 'valuable' if one has ever lived with 'not having'. The real enabler is 'valuable'."

(Dedicated to the self made)

"'Win' or 'lose', each has more or less the same meaning. The initial brings satisfaction and the latter creates the determination to be satisfied."

(Dedicated to The Olympics and all Olympians)

"The home of the wise is
decorated with wisdom."

(Dedicated to Kings and Queens of the realm)

"If you must remove everything from someone, leave that person with absolute love and s/he has it all. When you give absolute love, you remove nothing."

(In Love we find all)

"While thinking out of this world, the Earth keeps revolving on its axis, in the orbit, whilst lit by the Sun in places."

(Dedicated to all Astronauts and the morning Sun that greets my soul quite often)

"The closer you are to the ground, the more gravity you experience, but I think the less your ego. Try it with your shoes off on the beach. When nature makes contact we are naturally humble."

(Dedicated to the down-to-earth and the light-hearted)

"When you convey your vision to the world in the form of a theory, acceptance of your idea may not be immediate, but when its true and compelling values become unavoidable, the whole world will pay attention. The only guiding tools you need are; focus, determination and goodwill for humanity."

(Dedicated to Bill Gates)

"Thoughts are the master of Freewill.
They originate from our inner nature
and flow into the subjective mind, giving
us the full command of our Freewill.
Therefore to think, speak and act in
benefit
of humanity is immensely worthwhile."

(Dedicated to positive use of Freewill)

George D. Naike, F.R.C., MCIH.

"Success is not just about popularity. It is underpinned by a combination of that, compassion, genuine display of human feelings toward those in need, and some observe it very well."

(Dedicated to Jacqueline E. Henderson - KiiS 1065, Australia)

"Every waking moment is a continuation of our personal evolution. With time ticking we grow and renew. The phenomenon of sleep gives us a break from our daily lives, just as much as our waking state draws us closer (moment-by-moment) to the great respiratory power of sleep. Sleep is a necessity, not a possibility."

(Dedicated to the young and the restless)

GEORGE D. NAIKE, F.R.C., MCIH.

"The major advantage of using each
opportunity we have to serve humanity
is that we acquire certain wisdom
that is not readily perceivable
by the ordinary looking eyes."

(In memory of Nelson Mandela)

"Intelligence lives in our mental faculty. Its true nature can only be revealed through our words and, or, behaviour. Since it is inevitable that we speak and behave for our own survival, our thoughts and reasoning are the gateways through which we can shape, refine and deliver our speeches and actions for the greater good."

(In memory of Dr. Martin Luther King Jnr)

"We are blind to our reasoning faculty, literally. However, this indissociable and perfectly corresponding aspect of our being affords us all the necessary instincts of survival needed for a lifetime. Sometimes we need not see to believe because, Knowing when observed carefully, just as well, lines parallel with seeing proportions."

"Remembering is the natural flow forth of previously gained knowledge into our knowing at the present moment. It can also occur by the willful command of memory. It is the beautiful and necessary process of recollection where dwells hindsight."

(Dedicated to History and historians)

George D. Naike, F.R.C., MCIH.

"Ego opposes Altruism. It is virtually impossible to obtain a middle ground. No amount of rigor has yet produced such dynamic as Ego-altruistic, Altruistic–egoism, Egocentric-altruism..."

"When we remember a person, a place or a thing the image naturally flows into our realisation. If we apply love and positive emotions, we attune with that person (living or transitioned), place or thing."

(Keep positive mental pictures of your loved ones in mind, for when away)

"Just because you care, you rise up with the Sun and the works of your hands bring sweat to your brows. Day by day, you nurture the lands and tender the earth with paramount care. With you barter surely trades and without you pangs of hunger might flare to fore. You truly are the heroes of the Earth. I salute you with the Might of The Rain and Sunshine as you voyage toward your copious harvests."

(Dedicated to Farmers, Gardeners and Agriculture)

"Science recognises the so-called child prodigy as the one who displays unquestionable and exceedingly accelerated intelligence in one or more fields and, or, performance at a very young age. However, scientists, by the same token, cannot be entirely able to elucidate the reasons for such hastened faculties of such illuminated minds.

It is of special interest that such high level intelligence obviously does not result from some objectively compounded apprenticeship of some sort. Neither does it arrive from some vortex of information and knowledge physically divulged to the child from parents.

Whereas some try deploying extraordinary thinking trying to arrive at the "hows" and "whys" of such phenomenon, these extraordinarily gifted souls amongst us simply attribute their masterminds and prowess to Divine Grace."

(Dedicated to the young and gifted (past and present). With special emphasis on; Michelangelo (whose education could not be furthered, as he'd mastered the art of painting by the tender age of eight), Beethoven (and his Mastership of the Piano at just ten years old), Chelsea Dock (accomplished Pianist by age five), Mozart (who performed The Sonata at the very young age of just four), the physician Thomas Young (who spoke six languages at eight years of age), Mabou Louiseau (who spoke six languages and played the Harp, Clarinet, Violin, Drums, Guitar and Piano at seven years of age), the great Victor Hugo, one of the greatest poets that ever lived)...

To read about the author, please

- Search online for Balboa Press Bookstore
- Click on Balboa Press
- Enter Chiseled Intelligence into the search bar
- Book should display
- click on book and scroll down
- There you will find; Overview, About the Author ...
- Please read and kindly leave a comment

To purchase Ebook version of this work, Please visit Amazon.com ebooks or Balboa Press Books and search for Chiseled Intelligence.

"Genuine excellence is the selfless habits of kindness toward others." (GN-Copyright)

Thank you.

Printed in the United States
By Bookmasters